MW01595597

Shannon
Always
Think.
By
White

The Winning Edge: Goal Setting and Time Management
Copyright © 2011 by Greg White

Table of Contents

THE WINNING EDGE:
Goal Setting and
Time Management

By Greg White

Preface

Having the good fortune of being a college athlete and coaching college basketball, I have had the opportunity to be around young students daily for a number of years. Most college kids are energized with their daily activities, however several things separate high achievers from average and low achievers.

Work ethic can only take you so far. The real key to success is organization. Organization starts with proper use of time and one's ability to set goals. The student who rises to the top understands they have to take control of their time and not waste it.

It is my hope that this book can be a catalyst towards great achievement. There is no better feeling than setting a high goal and then doing the necessary things to achieve it. Work ethic, time management, and goal setting go hand in hand towards achieving amazing success. Good Luck!

Greg White

Part I

Goal Setting

Introduction to Goal Setting

Goal setting can provide numerous personal and professional advantages. However, many of us fail to take advantage of this tool. Without goal setting it can be difficult to attain your desires. It is far too easy to become distracted and sidetracked by outside forces. Goal setting gives you the discipline and control you need to harness your desires and use them to motivate yourself.

Ideally, goal setting should be performed on a routine basis. You have to personally decide what it is you want to accomplish, and then developing a step by step plan by which these goals can be obtained. Ultimately, goal setting allows you to develop a road map for where you want to go in life. Without goal setting, you are much more likely to wander around aimlessly.

Concrete goal setting requires real time and effort. You will also need to continuously update your goals, as old goals are accomplished and new desires form.

At first, you may not be able to see the difference goal setting can make in your life. However, sooner or later, the importance of goal setting will manifest itself.

Why Goal Setting is Important

With sharp, clearly defined goals you gain the ability to measure and take pride in what you have accomplished. By being able to take stock of all the hard work you have put into something, you can see the results of that work, which also serves to increase your self-confidence.

Goal setting likewise gives you the ability to focus your attention and organize your schedule in order to make the most of your time. This powerful technique provides many advantages, such as:

- Achieving more
- Improving performance
- Increasing your motivation to achieve
- Increasing your pride and satisfaction in your achievements
- Improving your self-confidence
- Eliminating attitudes that hold you back
- Eliminating unhappiness

Studies have indicated that people who use goal-setting effectively:
- Suffer less from stress and anxiety
- Concentrate better
- Show more self-confidence
- Perform better
- Are happier and more satisfied

The process of goal setting gives you the ability to see what you have accomplished as well as what you are capable of achieving. This translates into more confidence and a can-do attitude to achieve goals which appear to be difficult.

When beginning the process of goal setting, it is important to understand how goals work. If you are interested in setting goals to benefit you in school, your personal goal setting can benefit other people.

The goals you set should correlate with your personal values. Many people find it helpful to begin the goal setting process by defining their motivations in life. This is similar to a mission statement that most well grounded companies and organizations undertake.

Stand out by writing down words and sentences that you feel describe what you want out of life, the principles which guide you through life, and the things you want to achieve out of life.

Like most people, you probably fill more than one role in your life. These may be expressed as a wife or husband, grandparent, professional, volunteer, etc. Your mission statement may reflect these roles accordingly.

Setting Goals Effectively

The first thing you must understand about goals – in order to set them effectively, is that they are actually set on different levels.

The first step in that process is to decide what you want out of life and to pinpoint the overall goals you would like to achieve.

Next, those goals are broken down into smaller goals. These are the targets that you must hit in order to reach the larger, lifetime goals you have set.

The final step is to begin working on the plans you have determined necessary, in order to achieve those goals.

In order for your goals to be effective they must meet several guidelines:

Each goal must be positive in nature. Avoid negativity. For example, you might describe your goal as, "Maintain my diet this holiday season." instead of "Do not overeat this holiday season."

Goals must be precise. This means they must include a goal, date, time and amount so that they can be easily measured. This technique will allow you to gauge when the goal has been achieved. Upon achievement of the goal you will have the satisfaction of completing it.

Every goal you set must have a priority. This is especially important when you have set multiple goals. You can avoid feeling overwhelmed and will be able to direct your attention to goals which are most important at the time.

All goals must be written. The action of writing it down makes the plan concrete and motivates you to accomplish it.

If a goal feels too big, it should be kept small. This is very important because low-level goals are more achievable. Otherwise, you may feel as though you are making no progress and quickly want to abandon it. Goals that are small and incremental provide more opportunities for reward, and give you the drive you need to accomplish larger lifetime goals.

Avoid outcome goals. Instead, set performance goals. An example of an outcome goal is: "I will save some money." On the other hand, an example of a performance goal is: "I will save at least $20 from my next paycheck to put towards a vacation fund."

Always set goals which you have as much control and power over as possible. You can easily become discouraged by failing to meet a goal because of something that was beyond your control, whether it is bad weather, illness or just a series of unfortunate circumstances.

Goals should be personal. In today's society it can be easy to fall into the goals others have set for you – many of which are unrealistic. You must always keep your ambitions and desires uppermost in your mind, not those of others.

Take the time to understand the nature of your goal so that you do not make them unrealistic. You should also understand the obstacles which could prevent you from achieving your goal, as well as the skills which are necessary in order for you to achieve it.

On the other hand, goals should not be too low. Otherwise there is not much satisfaction in achieving them. Goals which are more challenging will give you more satisfaction when you achieve them.

Do not set goals that are unachievable. If you know that you are unlikely to achieve a goal, there is a strong chance that you won't put in the effort to try to do so.

With goal setting, you can decide which things are important for you to achieve and separate them from those that are irrelevant. Goal setting will also build your confidence and self-esteem when you look back on each successful milestone.

When you have achieved your goals, take time to enjoy those achievements. It is also important that you reward yourself appropriately. Enjoy your success!

As with any improvement process, it is critical that you perform a review of your goal setting. Analyze the portions of the process that were successful as well as those that were not. You can use this review to improve future performance.

The most successful people in the world recognize that defining your goals correctly leads to more achievements. This includes the wording, structure, format and timing.

How you use these elements to frame your goal will strongly affect its perceived difficulty.

Take a look at the following tips to help you frame your goals in a way in which you will be more likely to achieve success:

i. Always quantify measurements. If your goal is to save a specific amount of money, state your goals as "I want to save $150 this month" not "I want to save some money this month." If you save $2 this month then you have certainly saved some money, but that amount is far different than the specified goal.

ii. Keep your goals simple in nature. One of the stumbling blocks to creating attainable goals is making them too complex. By keeping your goals clear, simple and focused you will be able to achieve them.

iii. The goals you set must also be something that you care about. If you set a goal that does not matter to you, you are not likely to put much effort towards achieving it.

iv. Make it a point to ensure that your goals are rational. You must devise a plan for reaching your goals. If you set a goal that does not make sense then you are setting yourself up for failure before you even get started.

v. Goals should be tangible as well. It should not be something abstract. For example, you should not set a goal of becoming happier, but a goal that states "I want to buy a new car this year."

vi. Share your goals. One of the best ways that you can improve your chances of achieving your goals is by letting others who care about you know about it. When you have a support team, regardless of your goal, you are more likely to stick with it and do what you need to in order to succeed.

vii. Finally, never set goals that contradict the values that are important to you. If your goals and your values do not coincide, you will feel conflicted. By matching your goals with your values, you will be sure to find success.

Developing a Blueprint for Setting Goals

When first learning to set goals, it is important to develop a template or blueprint to help you in the process. Everyone's goals are different but it is essential to learn the necessary steps that will allow you to set goals successfully. A blueprint can serve as a checklist for future goal setting.

First, you should develop a deep desire to achieve your goal. If you already have an intense desire for the goal you have developed, then the rest should be easy.

Sometimes, you may have a goal that you know needs to be accomplished but you do not have a strong desire for it. However, you can motivate yourself by taking the time to sit down and write out all the benefits and advantages of completing this goal.

So, how many advantages and benefits should your list contain? The number may be unique for each individual, but at a minimum it should contain 20 benefits. In the beginning, it may seem difficult to come up with that many benefits, but you will be surprised at how quickly the list will come together once you start working on it. Like a snowball, it will gain momentum as it grows. As you see the list of advantages and benefits grow, your desire to accomplish the goal will likewise expand.

It is also important to make sure that the goal you set does not contradict with your values. Achieving your goals will be useless if you compromise your beliefs.

The next step will be to write down your goal. By writing down your goals they become substantial and concrete.

Be as specific as possible. When writing your goals it is not enough to simply say that you want to save some money, make more money or purchase new gadgets.

There is a tremendous difference between saying that you want to purchase a new gadget and stating that you want to purchase a new 32GB iPod touch.

You need to take the time to identify possible obstacles you need to overcome in order to accomplish your goal. Likewise, you also need to identify solutions to help you overcome these obstacles. These solutions may include knowledge, organizations or people.

Many people feel they work best under pressure. Set a deadline for your goal. This will help you to analyze where you are now in relation to the achievement of your goal and then measure how long you believe it will take you to complete the goal.

Do not set a deadline that is unreasonable. It is much better to set a deadline that is more attainable. Also remember to factor in time to deal with problems and make up for delays.

The next step in developing a blueprint is to create a plan. This means you need to list all activities related to the achievement of your goal and then prioritize them.

Once you have the list prioritized, rewrite it in priority order and make any corrections that are needed.

One technique that many people find to be quite helpful in visualizing their goals is to create a storyboard for their goals. This can be accomplished quite simply by purchasing an inexpensive piece of poster board and attaching photos related to your goal to the poster board. You can obtain suitable photos from a variety of sources, like magazines and brochures. As you view the collage everyday, you will be more likely to stay on track with the plans and tasks necessary to achieve that goal.

The final step in developing a blueprint for the accomplishment of your goals is to have persistence, resolve, and determination. You should never give up, even when you run into obstacles. Instead visualize how it will feel when you accomplish your goal and allow that to carry you through difficult periods.

Now that you have a blueprint for setting goals, it is time to look at the areas in your life where you can set goals. There are basically six areas of life where goals can be set.

Education and Knowledge
How are you doing in school? Do you feel inadequate with what you are learning in school? How do you see your life after high school?

Finance and Career
Do you enjoy your work? Do you feel you are making a contribution to society? Are you living up to your potential?

Social and Cultural

Does your circle of friends enrich your life and contribute to your sense of fulfillment and well-being? Is there at least one other person with whom you can discuss important life experiences? Do you have interests outside of your career and family (e.g., sports, theater, outdoor events)?

Spiritual and Ethical

Have you ever articulated specific personal values to yourself? Are you living up to those personal values?

Is religion important to you? If so, are you happy with the way you are practicing your religion? If not, have you reconciled your relationship with a higher power or with the universe in general?

Family and Home

Have you realized your dream in terms of your home and family relationships?

Physical and Health

How satisfied are you with your current level of physical health? Are you living up to your own standards in terms of diet and exercise? Are you fit enough to do the things you want to do?

Many people tend to focus on one area of their life when setting goals (such as financial and career) and virtually neglect the other areas of their life. This is very dangerous thinking.

One of the biggest problems with this type of strategy is that it does not give you a balanced life. Sure, you may end up accomplishing all of your financial goals but you may do so at the expense of your health, family, home and ethics.

By taking the time to ensure that you have goals set in the six major areas of your life, you will be able to have a balanced life that does not contradict with your values.

For some people, it can be difficult to look at goals five, ten, fifteen or more years from now. If you find yourself falling into that category, one way to overcome this is by defining the things that you want most this year.

Goals I want to Accomplish this Year 20_____
Family and Home
Spiritual and Ethical
Social and Cultural
Financial and Career
Physical and Health
Mental and Educational

Goal #7:
Goal #8
Goal #9
Goal #10

A technique that you can use to establish more long term goals is to think of the three most important things you want to accomplish before you die.

Take a look at this template to help you get started.

Goal #1:_____

Obstacles:_____
_____

Resources to overcome obstacles:
_____
_____
_____

Steps to Achieve goal:
_____
_____

Goal #2:_____
Obstacles:_____
_____
_____

Resources to overcome obstacles:
_____
_____
_____

Steps to Achieve goal:
_____
_____
_____

Goal #3:_____
Obstacles:_____
_____
_____

Resources to overcome obstacles:
_____
_____
_____

Steps to Achieve goal:
_____
_____
_____

After you have established goals for the ten most important things you want to accomplish this year and the three most important things you want to accomplish before you die, you can then begin working on lists of things that you want to accomplish within the next twenty years, ten years, five years and finally to the three most important things you want to accomplish within one day.

Motivation and Goal Setting Worksheet

1. What are your life time goals?

_____
_____
_____
_____

2. What are your goals for the next three to five years?

_____
_____
_____
_____

3. What are your goals for this coming year?

_____
_____
_____
_____

4. What are the things you need to do in order to accomplish this year's goals?

_____
_____
_____
_____

In some cases, you may find that the goals you set on a short term basis are actually activities that will allow you to accomplish more long term goals.

For example, saving a certain amount of money this month or year may allow you to save for the down payment you need to purchase a new home or car; which is a more long term goal.

When setting these goals it is important to establish the difference between wishing for things and actually setting a plan in action that will allow you to accomplish them.

What are the circumstances within which this goal will be realized?

Who _____

What _____

When _____

Where _____

Why _____

You also need to focus on the outcome of your goal in order to solidify it in your mind. Take a look at the following questions that can help you in this regard.

Q. What good will happen if you get the outcome?
A. _____

Q. What good will happen if you do not get the outcome?
A. _____

Q. What won't happen if you are successful?
A. _____

Q. What won't happen if you are unsuccessful?

A. _____

Q. Is there a reason that you might be hesitant to obtain the goal?

A. _____

Q. Is there any reason to believe that this idea will not work?

A. _____

While it is important that you have multiple goals set in six major areas of your life, it is also important that you only focus on one project at a time. At first this advice may seem a contradictory; however one of the biggest mistakes that people make in goal setting is trying to work on too many things at once.

This is where making a to-do list or goals for the day list can become extremely helpful. This type of list will help you to focus on the tasks that are important in order to accomplish the most pressing goals. While it may be more enjoyable to work on your goal of improving your golf game, this goal may not be as pressing or imperative as working on your goal to increase your sales so that you can achieve the promotion.

Prioritizing your goals requires you to actually sit down and rank them according to importance. For example, after you have set goals for the 10 most important things you want to accomplish this year, it will then be necessary to rank them according to importance.

When ranking your goals, consider factors such as which goals will contribute the most growth for you professionally/personally. You might consider adding a priority ranking of A, B or C to your list of goals. According to this priority system:

A: Goals that have the highest value and immediate concern
B: Goals that have medium value and secondary importance
C: Goals that have least value and importance

Chances are that when you have completed the ranking of your goals you will find that you have multiple priority A goals. In this case you will then need to separate them and rank them according to importance.

#1 PRIORITY: _____
(Time needed to complete_____)
Goals:
(_____) _____(____/____/____)
(_____) _____(____/____/____)
(_____) _____(____/____/____)
(_____) _____(____/____/____)
(_____) _____(____/____/____)

#2 PRIORITY: _____
(Time needed to complete_____)
Goals:
(_____) _____(____/____/____)
(_____) _____(____/____/____)
(_____) _____(____/____/____)
(_____) _____(____/____/____)
(_____) _____(____/____/____)

#3 PRIORITY: _____
(Time needed to complete_____)
Goals:
(_____) _____ (____/____/____)
(_____) _____ (____/____/____)
(_____) _____ (____/____/____)
(_____) _____ (____/____/____)
(_____) _____ (____/____/____)

#4 PRIORITY: _____
(Time needed to complete_____)
Goals:
(_____) _____ (____/____/____)
(_____) _____ (____/____/____)
(_____) _____ (____/____/____)
(_____) _____ (____/____/____)
(_____) _____ (____/____/____)

#5 PRIORITY: _____
(Time needed to complete_____)
Goals:
(_____) _____ (____/____/____)
(_____) _____ (____/____/____)
(_____) _____ (____/____/____)
(_____) _____ (____/____/____)
(_____) _____ (____/____/____)

After you have written a detailed plan for each goal, including the following:
- Specific details
- The unit of measurement you will use to assessment the achievement of your goal
- How your goal will be achieved
- Obstacles you will face in achieving your goal and resources you can use to overcome those obstacles

- Timeframe for achieving your goal

Define the steps necessary for you to accomplish your priority A goals. These activities should then be listed in sequential order. Determine how much time you will need to accomplish each of these activities, and then set a separate time frame for each activity.

A deadline is simply not enough for some people to stay on track, it is also a good idea to establish an exact start and finish date. This will help to ensure the completion of your goal and not give you unrealistic timeframe expectations.

Task:	Target Date:	Date Completed:

Do not forget to include milestones along the way to help you measure your success and ensure that you are on the right track. When setting milestones its important to also include information that can help you to determine what you expect to achieve by each milestone. Consider this as a sort of goal setting check-up.

Now that you have your overall goals set, prioritized them, and have a list of activities that are necessary in order for you to complete those goals, it is time to develop a daily and weekly schedule. You can do this by reviewing the list of activities you have drafted and their corresponding timeframes.

Many people find it helpful to check off activities as they complete them on the path to achieving their goals. This can provide you with a sense of definite accomplishment and prevent you from feeling as though you are not doing enough to accomplish your goals (especially long term goals).

When you are performing check-ups for your goal it is also important to perform evaluations to determine whether your goals are still realistic and obtainable. You may find it is necessary to make some adjustments in order to compensate for other factors. In some cases you may find you need to adjust your timeline in order to compensate for events outside your control and caused delays.

Weekly Plan
Date:

Activities Required to Accomplish Objectives	Priority	Time Needed	Day

Forming Goal Statements

Now that you have a clear idea of how goals are set it is time to actually get down to the business of setting your goals. The first step in the process is forming a goal statement. The success and failure of your goal depends on how you form your goal statement, so it is important to formulate it clear and accurate.

While this may seem to be a daunting task at first, it becomes quite easy when you follow a simple plan. This plan is referred to by many life coaches as the SMART acronym. SMART stands for:

Specific

Measurable

Action-Oriented

Realistic

Time and Resource Constrained

First, all goals you set should be specific enough so you always know exactly what it is you are working toward. Your goals should also be measurable so you are able to determine when your goal has been achieved.

In terms of action, your goal should have activities attached to it that will produce results and finally your goal should be timely with a definitive timeline for completion.

Let's take a look at a few examples of goal statements to begin seeing how statements can either fit this profile or fall outside of it.

"Purchase a new computer."
"Purchase a Macbook Pro with 250 GB hard drive."

"I want to make a lot of money."
"I want to increase my annual income to $15,000 within the next five years."

"I want to own a Nissan GT-R"
"I want to purchase a pre-owned Nissan GT-R within the next two years."

"I want to save money for a trip to abroad."
"I want to save $2,000 for a trip to Costa Rica."

"I want to have better grades."
"I want to raise my GPA to 3.5 this semester."

As you can see there is a huge difference between forming a goal statement that is vague and forming a goal statement that is specific, measurable, action oriented and time constrained.

Rather than use the SMART acronym, some people find it more beneficial to pose a series of questions to each of their goal statements. Questions that can help you evaluate the effectiveness of your goal statement include:

What will be different when I achieve this goal? If you do not foresee any major changes in your life after achieving this goal, you need to go over it and revise your goal statement.

How will I know I have achieved this goal when I see it? You must be able to determine when your goal has been accomplished. For example, when saving money, there is a significant difference between saving $5 and $500,000 even if both scenarios meet the original goal statement.

What is the optimum performance level of this goal? If you do not take care to set a performance level for your goal, there may be a strong temptation to not perform as well as you can to achieve it.

What constraints, if any, might affect the performance of this goal? As always, it is important to define any obstacles you may encounter when setting your goals so you know what you need to overcome in order to achieve it.

When defining your goal statements, it is also important to take a look at the exact terminology you use. Avoid using words that are clearly vague in nature such as the following:

Appreciate	Recognize
Attitude	Hear
Familiar with	Interest in
Feelings for	Knowledge of
Capable of	Listen to
Conscious of	Adjust to
Confidence in	Responsive to
Experience	Think
Attitude	Understand
Realize	

Consider the following goal statement template:

"I commit to having _____ on or before _____by doing _____ and because _____."

The Difference between Dreams and Goals

When beginning to set your goals it is important to understand both the connection as well as the significant differences between dreams and goals. Most people have dreams and daydreaming is a favored hobby among a large portion of the population. However, some individuals achieve their dreams while others do not.

That difference is goal setting. It turns an aimless dream into a driven goal. You can significantly increase the odds of achieving your dream, no matter how unattainable it may seem at the time to you, by clarifying it, providing specific details, defining it so you can see it, feel it and know it when you see it.

Even if you feel a dream is too difficult to achieve, you can improve your chances by defining it as a goal. This makes it concrete and helps to assure that opportunities will not go by unnoticed.

The process of goal setting also gives you a step by step plan so that you know exactly what you need to do in order to achieve your dream. It helps you to avoid detours and dead ends that might distract and delay you on the way to achieving that dream.

What Makes Up a Good Goal?

Realizing the difference between good goals and harmful goals is of utmost importance. A good goal is a goal that is written, challenging, believable, specific, measurable, and contains a specific deadline, while a harmful goal is a complete waste of time.

When writing your goals, you have to recognize the numerous options available to you. The most traditional method is the pen and paper method and this works quite well for many people. If it helps, use a word processing program or any other software you find helpful for writing down your goals. The important point here is they need to be written down.

The goal must be believable by you. At the very least this does not necessarily mean others must believe your goal. In fact, in many cases you may find there are numerous people who will not believe you can accomplish your goal. This does not make the goal any less achievable or worthy. It simply may mean you need to work a little harder at achieving it.

It is important when setting your goals to make them challenging. All of your goals should not be so simple that you do not need to exert effort in order to achieve them. There is very little satisfaction or accomplishment in achieving goals of this nature.

However, not all of your goals need to be challenging. One of the steps necessary in order to complete a larger long term goal is to accomplish smaller, easier goals along the way.

One of the great things about easy goals is they build a sense of follow-through, responsibility and reward. They also allow you to feel the joy of gratification for your efforts.

While not all goals must be challenging, all goals should be measurable and specific. This means they should not be vague or ambiguous so you do not know when they have been completed.

One of the new trends in goal setting may dictate that goals no longer need a deadline; however, it still remains true most people work better when there is a specific deadline in place. This allows you to know exactly how much time you have remaining in which to complete your goal and perform periodic check-ups along the way.

There is a fine line between establishing goals that are challenging and realistic. Ideally, a goal should be both but it can admittedly be difficult to determine when a goal fits both of these criteria.

If the majority of the goals you set are not realistic, you run the very real risk of becoming frustrated and disappointed when you are not able to accomplish them. This does not mean you should not attempt goals that seem very challenging or that defy what appear to be the odds. Some of the most successful people in the world have done just that and obtained the goals they sought. Just make sure you have a good balance.

All goals should be broken down into smaller, more manageable goals that can be worked on individually. This will prevent you from becoming overwhelmed. These smaller goals are often referred to as baby steps and they are a great way to build confidence and a solid track record.

Tips for Dealing with Obstacles in Goal Setting

There are several areas in the goal setting process you need to watch out for in order to avoid obstacles. Let's take a look at a few.

It is important you remain focused on the goals you have set for yourself. One way to do this is by avoiding the temptation to set too many goals at one time.

While there is nothing wrong with having a large number of goals going at the same time, you can quickly run into trouble if several of those goals are due at the same time. Be realistic in the amount of time you can dedicate to each goal.

At the same time, it is important not to limit yourself by only assigning simple and easy goals. Always make it a point to be working on one simple goal and one difficult goal at any given time. As these goals are accomplished, you will become motivated by your own success, which will then spur you on to accomplishing other goals.

Likewise, make it a point to be working on at least one short term goal and one long term goal. The short term goals are usually simpler in nature and will give you the confidence you need to accomplish more difficult goals. Long term goals are those that generally will require two years or longer in order to complete. Goals that require less time than this to complete can be categorized as a short term or mid-range goal.

When setting your goals make sure you are setting performance goals and not outcome goals. Outcome goals can quickly lead to disappointment because the goal is focused on the end result and not the performance. This type of goal is too easily affected and influenced by reasons out of your control.

Always be realistic in the goals you set. The general rule of thumb is if you cannot even believe in your goal then there is virtually almost no chance you will be able to achieve it.

Do not give in to the temptation to set goals so low there is really no sense of accomplishment, or benefit in achieving them. Always work on goals that are challenging to you.

The importance of setting goals that are specific and clear cannot be stressed enough. It can be difficult to know when you have achieved vaguely defined goals because these types of goals are difficult to measure.

It is important to prioritize not only your goals but the action steps required to accomplish your goals. When you are prioritizing your goals, you also need to be flexible. When necessary, change due dates or put a goal on hold if you need to make changes.

As you work with goal setting you will probably start to notice it is possible to combine certain goals and tasks. Whenever possible, it is a good idea to do this. This is good time management and it will allow you to achieve more in less time.

Finally, make it a point to be balanced in all you do. Work on setting goals in the six major areas of your life. Always be sure your goals do not conflict with your own values.

The Ten Basic Rules of Goal Setting

Rule # 1: Be Decisive in your goal setting.

The responsibility for making all decisions relating to your goals ultimately resides with you. Decide early on what you want, why you want it and what needs to be done in order to obtain it.

Rule # 2: Stay focused

It can be very easy to get sidetracked in the process of obtaining your goals, especially when dealing with long term goals. It will always be your ability to maintain a strong focus that determines whether you are able to achieve your goals or not.

Rule #3: Be Open to Failure

It is quite one thing to be confident in your abilities and another to be able to accept that failure is a part of life. By learning to accept failure, you are able to evaluate it objectively and learn from it.

Rule #4: Always Write Down your Goals

When a goal is not written down it is far too easy to push it to the far recesses of your mind when your life becomes burdened with other matters. Take the opportunity to create success for yourself by writing down your goals and committing them to an action plan.

Rule #5: Plan for your goals

No goals can be accomplished without planning. Without proper planning, you can always expect to fail more times than you will succeed.

Rule # 6: Get others involved

One of the best things about achieving a goal is in sharing the success of that moment with others. When you allow others to become involved in your goals, you not only provide others with wisdom and knowledge to help them in their own goals, you give yourself your own personal cheering section.

Rule # 7: Take action

Goals cannot be achieved without action. You must divide your goals up into tasks you can accomplish or your goals will always remain distant dreams.

Rule #8: Reward yourself

History has shown that people naturally respond better when there is an incentive at stake. Think of things that will give you pleasure when you accomplish even small goals. Take the time to enjoy your success and reward yourself for your persistence, dedication and hard work.

Rule # 9: Do not forget to review your goals

Performing reviews along the way is the best way to maintain a healthy goal system. This allows you to be proactive and discover any small problems before they become major obstacles.

Rule #10: Always maintain your personal integrity

This rule cannot be stressed enough. It is imperative you maintain your personal integrity and never set goals that will conflict with your own personal values.

Exercises in Goal Setting

Exercise 1: Writing a goal statement

Write a brief summary statement of a goal you would like to accomplish. Be sure to include such factors and details as cost, timing, location, etc. Be as specific as possible.

Goal Statement:

_____
_____
_____

Exercise 2: Measure of success and goal assessment

The measure of success is knowing when you have achieved your goal and to what degree your goal has been achieved.

Write specific, measurable statements for possible outcomes. Whenever possible give yourself a range of results that will allow you to stay motivated and not become disappointed by just barely missing your goal. This method also allows you to take advantage of continuous improvement.

Measure of Success for goal:

_____
_____
_____

Exercise 3: List the major tasks needed to achieve the goal.

Do not allow yourself to become too weighed down with details. One way to do this is by working backwards from the achievement of your goal to the first step needed to accomplish the goal. This is a great way to break large goals down into manageable chunks.

Tasks Necessary to Accomplish Goal:

_____

_____

_____

_____

_____

_____

Exercise 4: Prioritizing

Make a point to spend some time assigning priority ratings to the tasks that need to be accomplished. Determine how much time is needed to complete each task and then prioritize the tasks so you always know what you need to be working on.

Weekly Plan
Date:

Activities Required to Accomplish Objectives	Priority	Time Needed	Day

Exercise 5: Timing

The process of assigning real dates as deadlines for completing activities can increase your success rate. If you do not already have one, make it a point to pick up a calendar or datebook and assign timelines to your tasks according to realistic expectations.

Exercise 6: Assess your desire for this goal

When considering taking on a new goal, it is important you evaluate the level of your desire to accomplish this new goal. Likewise, you must also spend some time in determining whether you have the resources necessary to accomplish it.

Ability (skill)

Have I been taught to do this?

Do I see this as my role?

Do I know how to do this?

Have I successfully done this, or something similar, before?

Enthusiasm (will)

Do I want to do this? Does it correspond with my personal values?

What is the risk of failure? Am I comfortable with that risk of failure?

Do I believe I can do it?

Exercise 7: Evaluate your Goals

Always use the SMART model to evaluate your goals as well as take the time to determine what could have been done differently. Keep this in mind the next time you set out to achieve a similar goal so you will be more successful.

Evaluating Goals

Remember each goal you set should meet the SMART system.

Specific

Measurable

Action-Oriented

Realistic

Time and Resource Constrained

Specific

All goals should be straightforward and specific. They should emphasize what it is that you want to happen and clearly define what it is you are going to do to accomplish that goal. Remember to concentrate on the following when creating specific goals:

What?
Why?
How?

WHAT are you going to do? Focus on using action words such as direct, organize, coordinate, lead, develop, plan, build, etc.

WHY is this goal important to accomplish at this time? What do you want to ultimately accomplish?

HOW are you going to do it? List down the steps you intend to do to achieve this goal.

Measurable

If you can't measure a goal then you won't be able to manage it. You will frequently need to divide your goals up into smaller segments, so this portion of the SMART model is very important. You need to be able to measure small term goals in order to accomplish the overall larger goal.

Take the time to establish concrete criteria for measuring progress toward the attainment of the goal. This will allow you to stay on track and reach your target dates.

Attainable

When you set goals that are out of your reach, it is quite likely that you will either be disappointed when you are not able to reach them or you won't even commit to trying to reach them at all. You will be able to give the process of obtaining your goals your best when you know that the goal is within your reach (even if it is challenging).

Realistic

Setting a realistic goal is not the same as setting an easy goal. In order for a goal to be realistic you must have the time and resources available in order to accomplish it. Obtaining the necessary resources may be one of the obstacles you will need to overcome, but you should be able to realistically do this. Be balanced in setting realistic goals. Remember that goals that are too difficult only set you up for failure, while goals that are too easy provide only a limited amount of accomplishment.

Timely

Always make it a point to set timeframes for your goals, whether this is in terms of days, weeks, months or even years. Put a specific ending point on it so that you have a target to work towards.

When evaluating your goals, it is also important to take a look at what has worked in the process and what could be improved for future goal projects. Consider these questions as evaluation tools:

1. What supports/resources worked best to help me achieve my goal(s)?
2. What problems did I encounter and how did I overcome them?
3. What progress did I make?
4. Was the timeframe I set to attain my goal(s) too fast or too slow?
5. Which objectives are still unmet?
6. What experiences did I find rewarding?
7. Which experiences were unrewarding?
8. Is the program working for me? Why or why not?
9. What recommendations can I make?

	Goal	How I did	The best thing about trying to reach this goal
1st			
2nd			
3rd			

The Importance of Belief in Accomplishing Goals

It is common for most of us to have some self-doubt that tells us that we can and cannot accomplish. In some people that doubt is stronger than others, and that can be detrimental to the process of goal setting. The success rate of our goals depends upon how we respond to that voice.

Believing in your own ability to accomplish what seems impossible is the key element to success. Even that negative voice inside your head can be changed by your own belief. It is your positive outlook that will increase your self-esteem and keep you focused on your goals.

Remember to never give up, always remain persistent and focused and above all, believe in your ability to attain your dreams.

Now that you have learned about goal setting, it is now time to put them to action! Put your learning to the test as you read through the basics of time management.

Part II

Time Management

Introduction to Time Management

"No one has enough time, but everyone has all there is."

For many students, the need for time management is not realized until they begin their first semester in college, and discover that they no longer have the security of highly structured schedules. Where teachers once handled the details of structured assignments, the university life presents a wide open field for students, in a kind of swim or sink environment.

With more freedom, flexibility, and less time required to attend class, but far more home work expected, students frequently find themselves in trouble when balancing their schedules and numerous extra-curricular commitments. If time management skills have not been honed up to this point, there is no better time than college to do it.

People have problems with time management for a wide variety of issues. In some cases it is simply because they are unaware that there are techniques out there that can help them to better utilize their time. Other individuals admittedly do not have the drive to implement a planning system into their lives or enjoy the 'rush' of working under pressure and meeting tight deadlines.

Unfortunately, the problem with this style of 'time management' is that it leads to stress, failed projects and ultimately a lower sense of self-worth.

Despite the many issues surrounding poor time management, many students fail to implement a time management and scheduling program because they fail to see the advantages of such a program. The most common excuse for failure to plan is simply that it takes too much time to do so. Irony aside, there are numerous advantages to time management, and it is important to consistently set aside time to take care of this.

While it does require some effort to set up and continually maintain a time management program, the most important advantage of doing so is that you will immediately gain time. A time management program will also help to motivate and inspire you as you begin to initiate your goals. Failure to plan often leads to procrastination and ultimately stress. Implementing a time management program in your life will help to reduce avoidance, eliminate last minute cramming and reduce stress and anxiety.

In the following pages, we will present some of best known tips to help students get a handle on their schedules and begin efficiently managing their time. Once these skills are learned they can be applied to any job or career in the future.

Managing your Time

One of the most important things to understand to efficiently manage your time is that there are many ways to accomplish this. In order for you to manage your time efficiently, you must be aware of what is most important to you. In other words, what are your goals and how do you prioritize them?

It is important to begin the process of developing an internal schedule. Everyone, yourself included, works best in a given manner. You've most likely heard of so called morning people and those who are referred to as night owls. Each individual works best according to their own personal body clock.

It is critical that you learn early on, what works for you, and what does not. Do not fall into the trap of believing that simply because a schedule works for someone else; it will work for you as well. Take the time to find out peak periods and you'll quickly learn that it becomes much easier to handle both the tasks that are required of you and those that are important to you.

It is also important to understand how well you need to plan and how much improvement you need to begin managing your time efficiently.

Below are several questions to help you make this self-assessment. It is important that you answer each question honestly based on your own feelings, rather than what you think the 'right' answer may be.

	Never	Seldom	Sometimes	Often	Always
1. Do you make a to-do list?	Never	Seldom	Sometimes	Often	Always
2. Are you flexible with your plans?	Never	Seldom	Sometimes	Often	Always
3. How often do you accomplish what you plan?	Never	Seldom	Sometimes	Often	Always
4. Do you plan for things that are personally important to you?	Never	Seldom	Sometimes	Often	Always
5. Do you make plans in order to keep things in your life under control?	Never	Seldom	Sometimes	Often	Always
6. How often are your plans hindered by interruptions?	Never	Seldom	Sometimes	Often	Always

How to Score:

For questions 1-5, award yourself 1 point for each Never; 2 points for each Seldom, 3 points for each Sometimes, 4 points for each Often and 5 points for each Always. For question 6, award yourself 5 points for Never, 4 points for Seldom, 3 points for Sometimes, 2 points for Often and 1 point for Always.

Tally your points and check below to discover your current planning assessment.

6 - 10 The bad news is that you are not engaged in any sort of active planning. The good news is that it isn't too late to begin developing healthy new habits that can help you in efficiently managing your time.

11 – 15 While it appears that you currently engage in some type of planning system, there is a need to use it more efficiently.

16 – 20 On the surface, the planning system you are currently utilizing appears to be working, but there is a need for improvement in order to help handle interruptions and prioritize your activities.

21 – 25 Congratulations! You have a good handle on how to plan and prioritize your activities. Remember to do a periodic check-up to ensure that your goals continue to be met.

26 – 30 At this point it is important to be careful to learn the difference between good planning and obsessive control. Remember that some activities are out of your control and don't stress the small stuff.

Now that you have a basic understanding of where you may be on the planning playing field, it is time to get started with the basics of successful time management. As with any other task, there are certain tasks that are considered to be basic elements.

The first step is to set specific and definable goals for yourself. These goals can be both academic and personal.

Once your goals have been set, it is time to create a schedule around your academic calendar. For example, if your school is on a semester basis (most are) then you would begin by drafting a semester calendar; making sure you have reflected any major events such as major projects, term papers, etc.

After your calendar has been drafted you can begin to drill that schedule down by creating a weekly schedule. This schedule will reflect all activities that you are responsible for on a weekly basis; including your classes, meetings, lab work, club activities, etc.

Next it is important for you to understand your own body clock and peak periods. This will be very important as you begin to plan for specific time in order for you to work on each course and activity.

Finally, you will need to create a to-do list for each day. This list should ideally be created the night before so that you have an idea on how the following day should take shape.

If your day runs long, you may need to create your to-do list before or during breakfast. This is fine as long as it is done. Making a to-do list for the day gives you an idea of the things you need to do and how much time you must allot to each task.

Appendix A is an example of a master daily schedule. You can purchase blank calendars in an office supply store or your own college bookstore. You can also create your own on a word processing program. Remember, that you do not need to get too technical with the schedule; it is the content that matters.

How much time do you need to spend on your scheduling and how do you prioritize your activities? While balancing your activities and tasks required is no walk in the park, it IS possible.

One of the most common mistakes of scheduling is ironically trying to plan too far ahead. Whenever possible, it is always best to plan for only what already exists and then to add to your schedule only as events and activities pop up.

As a college student, the first activities that should appear on your schedule are your classes. You also need to plan study time for each course. When these activities have been planned, you can then begin to add in additional activities such as club meetings, outside work, eating times, travel and finally recreation.

Remember that your main job during the week consists of your classes; it is best to keep your recreation time restricted to the weekends.

Scheduling often results in disaster for college students for a variety of reasons. Below is a list of tips to help you avoid the most common traps for failing at time management.

- Get into the habit of thinking of your time as a precious commodity.
- Even mundane, routine tasks that you find displeasing can be easier to handle when you find at least one thing enjoyable about it.
- Get in the habit of reviewing your monthly calendar to anticipate how you might be able to better schedule your activities and time.
- Reward yourself for important tasks accomplished.
- Do not make exceptions and do not skip around. Do first things first.
- If you find yourself avoiding a task or activity, face it head on and get it over with.

- Whenever possible, set deadlines
- Do not allow pride to be your downfall. If you need help or advice, ask for it.
- Work on having an optimistic attitude and to see the good in all things.
- Always be on the look out for ways to expand upon your successes.
- Do not cry over spilled milk! Instead of regretting your failures, make a point to learn from your mistakes.
- Do not put yourself in a position where you miss out on the important things in life. Remember that if it is important to you; it is important to find the time to do it.
- Always be on the lookout for ways to free up your time.
- Always carry a small notepad or calendar with you so that you can write down reminder notes.
- At the end of each day, review the tasks you needed to accomplish and evaluate your progress. Make adjustments where necessary.

Students frequently comment that they do not have the time to accomplish the goals and activities that interest them most because they are too caught up in the activities that are required of them. Remember, if it is important to you: you should take the time to plan for it. Begin by recording any special activities you need to do or want to do on a regular basis.

To avoid being caught unprepared for your classes, be sure to schedule a preview time (5-30 minutes) immediately before each class. During the preview, review at least some of your notes in preparation for the upcoming class.

In addition, try to schedule a review time immediately after your classes (5-30 minutes) as well. This time can be used to edit and summarize your notes as well as look over any assignments that were given during the class and start planning on how you can accomplish them.

Along with your mini-reviews and regular study time, make a point to schedule intensive study/ review time for each class. At a minimum, you should try to schedule time each day for each class. Remember that you can learn more effectively by studying in regular, shorter sessions rather than trying to cram it all in during long study sessions.

You may also find that you are more efficient and at your best when you try to study the same subjects at the same time each study day. This type of routine can help you to develop a pattern; which will help you become a more efficient and effective learner.

Numerous studies indicate that regular exercise helps to reduce stress and tension; while helping you to feel better about yourself and what you can accomplish. Even if you are already taking a physical education class, be sure to schedule time each day or evening for physical activity.

Do not over plan. Be flexible in your scheduling and leave some blocks of time open for personal or academic needs as they arise.

Finally; allow time to relax and unwind. While this is best reserved for the weekends; it is an important part of surviving the college experience. Look at it as a reward for all the hard work you've put in during the week and for sticking to your schedule.

Below are several examples of different schedules, to help you come up with an idea of how to efficiently manage your time. Note that these schedules are based on weekly and long-term formats (such as term). While there is no need to use these exact formats; make it a point to not only plan for the present but the future as well.

Creating a Master Weekly Schedule

This activity allows you to account for all fixed and regular activities that remain the same for most of the semester. Begin by entering the following information:

- Enter your course schedule.
- Enter other routine meetings and responsibilities (e.g., work, church, sports practice, etc.)
- Enter routine mealtime, travel time, sleep, exercise, laundry, shopping, cleaning, etc.
- Enter regular times for recreation (social hobbies, athletics, private time, etc.)

After your Weekly Master schedule is complete, you can construct a regular weekly schedule. Some students find it helpful to plan their activities in blocks of 50 minutes each. This gives you the opportunity to follow each block with a 10 minute break.

Refer to Table 1.1 in Appendix B for the chart.

Creating a Semester Calendar

When planning your semester calendar, it is important to keep all items from your regular weekly schedule, as well as add in any other events that you expect will occur during the semester.

These events might include concerts or movies you would like to attend, trips home to visit your family, trips out of town with friends, sporting events, etc. Also include academic events such as meeting dates, project dates, due dates for exams, etc.

Refer to Table 1.2 in Appendix B for the chart.

Creating a Four Year Calendar

Creating a calendar that will take you through the length of your academic career is also very important and is one of the cornerstones of long range planning.

When handling this type of schedule, be sure to include the following types of activities

- All relevant courses you are taking or plan to take
- Trips and vacations
- Internships
- Employment

Refer to Table 1.3 in Appendix B for the chart.

Creating a To-Do list

We'll go into a little more detail regarding to-do lists later, but for now we'll cover some of the basics. Creating a to-do list is an easy and simple way to transfer important items from any schedule to a list that can be easily accessed.

You may find that it works better for you to create your list the night before or to write it down in the morning. Whichever method you prefer, you can start by using a 3x5 card that can easily fit into your pocket. Refer to your weekly schedule and jot down activities that have priority for today.

As these activities are completed, you can cross them off. Any activities that are not completed should be carried over to the next day. Although, a word of caution on the latter; too much of this can get you into a serious time constraint. Aim for what you can realistically accomplish.

Setting Goals and Priorities

As previously mentioned, when learning to manage your time it is important to not only commit the activities and tasks that are required of you to paper, but also to begin developing a statement of your long-range goals.

The long-term and four year planning calendars are one way to begin doing this; however, in order to maximize the effectiveness of this type of planning you must be explicit and specific in your goal statements.

In goal setting, you will do much more than simply state "This is what I want to do in _____ amount of time." You must also set shorter range goals that will help you to meet your long term goals. Prioritize the specific steps necessary for you to accomplish those goals.

One of the most difficult aspects of drafting long term plans is in understanding where to begin and then how to drill them down to manageable tasks. Below is an example of a long term goal and the intermediate and short term goals that are related.

Long-Term Career Goal: Career as a Physician (10 to 12 years).

Intermediate Career Goals:

- Enter and complete residency program. (3 to 5 years).
- Medical School (3 years).
- Bachelor's degree (4 years)

Short-Term Personal Goals: (Present):

- Major in Biology.
- Courses in biology, chemistry and anatomy and physiology.
- At least a 3.5 average for medical school.
- Volunteer work at local hospital.
- Volunteer or paid work as a research assistant (to generate reference letters from faculty).
- Study skills course to improve grades and study habits.
- Find a part-time job this summer to begin saving for medical school.

Daily, Weekly, and Semester Scheduling

The key to successful time management is in not only planning your daily and weekly schedule, but also in ensuring that you have developed a schedule for your obligations each semester. By constantly being aware of tasks looming on your semester schedule, you will be more likely to stick your weekly and daily schedule in order to remain on track with your plans.

One way to handle planning your daily activities is to simply make a list of everything that you both want and need to accomplish throughout the day. This type of schedule works very well for a daily planning tool; however, it can also be modified to cover other periods of time as well.

Priority can be handled in a number of ways; such as either numerically or alphabetically. For example 1= Highest Priority, 2= Moderate Priority, 3= Lowest Priority or likewise with an alphabetical system; A = Highest Priority, B = Moderate Priority, C = Lowest Priority.

Take a look at the sample schedule below:

Monday

1. Review notes for anatomy and physiology class. (A)
2. Study for biology class. (C)
3. Work out at the gym. (B)
4. Meet girlfriend for dinner. (A)
5. Write an e-mail to parents. (C)
6. Fraternity meeting (C)
7. Library research (B)

This type of schedule allows for a great deal of flexibility by committing to a balanced schedule that allows for academic activities as well as personal interests.

Regardless of what system you use to prioritize your tasks, it is essential that you commit the activities to paper. You may either purchase a calendar or planner for such purpose or simply write them down on a notebook or note card that you can carry with you throughout the day.

If you are the type of person that needs more structure, the hour by hour schedule mentioned and presented in the previous sections works very well for this purpose. Just be realistic in your scheduling. Make sure you schedule time for recreation and free time. Failure to do so can quickly lead to burn out and a complete abandonment of the system.

Balance

Every schedule, regardless of style or design, must have balance. Every student, no matter what their personal desires and goals may be, need a balanced life-style in order to be efficient, successful and happy.

When you fail to design a balanced schedule for yourself, your very health will reflect it. Many college students succumb to health problems because they put their personal wellbeing as their last priority. Remember to pay attention to following important areas of your life in order to avoid this trap:
1. Physical (exercise, nutrition, sleep)
2. Intellectual (cultural, aesthetic)
3. Social (intimate and social relationships)
4. Career (school and career goal directed work)
5. Emotional (expression of feelings, desires)
6. Spiritual (quest for meaning)

You do not necessarily need to schedule activities for every one of these areas (certainly not every day). However if you fail to take care of one of these areas in your life, you are definitely setting yourself up for trouble.

Procrastination, Distractions, and Other Problems

Two big problems with many time management and scheduling plans are distraction and procrastination. Not only are short-term goals compromised, but long term goals as well. For example, if you fail to study for your biology class and flunk out, it becomes much more difficult for you to get into medical school and eventually achieve your long term goal of becoming a doctor.

To avoid these types of problems, take a look at the following tips:

1. Ask for help and cooperation from those around you. Allow your spouse, family members, roommate, and others know about your efforts to manage time.
2. Allow for flexibility.
3. Be realistic in your planning approach and do not set yourself up for failure.
4. Make sure you jot down your schedules and priorities on paper.
5. Review your long-term and intermediate goals often. Keep a list where you will see it often.
6. Regularly eliminate unnecessary tasks that are not related to your goals or to maintaining a balanced life style.
7. Take advantage of your natural cycles, schedule the most difficult activities when you are at your best.
8. Learn to say "No" to people, including spouses, friends, children, and parents.
9. Reward yourself for effective time management.

Strategies for Time Management

Skills that will help you to better manage your time will continue to evolve throughout most of your life. Like any other skill set, you need to spend time practicing these skills in order to hone them.

Take advantage of your own natural biological rhythms. Biological rhythm refers to the times of day when your energy levels are at their highest and when you can accomplish your most important work.

If you are a morning person, do not put off important activities until late in the evening. Reserve your low energy periods for tasks that do not require much concentration, such as doing your laundry.

Create a situation in which you can more efficiently manage your tasks and activities by optimizing your work environment.

Give some thought to how you work best. Do you prefer to have music playing while you work or do you consider it to be a distraction? Take these things into consideration when designing your work environment.

Developing Priorities

Developing priorities is critical to any successful time management program. Without priorities it can be difficult to get anything accomplished or focus on the most critical tasks.

Create a personal set of priorities, ask yourself the following questions.

- What is the purpose of the job?
- What are the measures of success?
- What is exceptional performance?
- What kind of job is this?
- How do you achieve this?
- What are the priorities and deadlines?
- What resources are available?
- What costs are acceptable?
- How does this relate to other people?
- What is the broader picture within which you have to work?

The following steps can help you prioritize the tasks and activities you must accomplish.

Start by developing an overview of everything that you want to accomplish. Determine the time frame you'd like to work with. This may be on a long term basis such as a semester, an intermediate basis such as a month or on a short term basis such as a week or a day.

Be sure to include not only your academic but your personal goals as well; such as spending more time friends or family, playing sports or keeping fit, or even catching the big sale at the mall. Whatever your goals may be for your specified time frame, write them on separate index cards.

Next, organize your goals according to their priority. Determine the urgency of each goal that you have set and then separate them into two stacks; one stack for those goals that you have determined to be urgent and another for those that you deem to be non-urgent. For example, studying for an upcoming exam and catching the sale at the mall may be more urgent than other tasks because of deadlines that are attached to these goals.

Take the stack of urgent goals and further divide them into two categories: one representing items that are important and another representing items that are non-important. Do the same with the stack of non-urgent goals.

This type of method will help you to determine the priority of your goals and which are deemed to be important and urgent versus important but non-urgent. By setting priorities you can devote more time and energy to accomplishing the tasks that are important and urgent without wasting critical time on low priority tasks.

Regardless of what type of system you use, it is critical that you look ahead. Failure to look ahead and anticipate pitfalls can lead you to being caught unaware and forcing yourself to neglect other goals in order to cram for the most urgent one.

Many students attempt to ignore certain activities in order to create more time for themselves. This almost never works and always catches up with you. Failure to get enough sleep for example, will always result in negative side effects. If you allow your laundry to pile up you will have nothing appropriate to wear on the day of your big presentation. Skip enough meals and you'll soon find yourself in the emergency room.

Always allow room for flexibility. Some things are just going to occur that you have no control over. Leave enough room in your schedule to adjust your plans for unexpected events.

Procrastination

One of the biggest problems for college students is procrastination. Sometimes you may not even be aware that you are already procrastinating. At first glance, they can appear to be valid reasons for putting off your work. For example:

- "One more day won't make any difference; I'll just put that off until tomorrow."
- "It won't matter if I'm a few minutes late; no one else will be on time."
- "I work best under pressure."
- "I'll watch just 15 more minutes of TV."
- "I can't start on this paper until I know just how I want the first paragraph to read."

Procrastination can take on many forms, but in its essence it involves putting off tasks that you should be doing now. While you may have very good intentions of accomplishing the task later; there is very little chance this will happen. If you do return to the task, there's a high likelihood that you will give it less than your best because you waited for the last minute.

Procrastination occurs for a number of different reasons. The most common are waiting for the right mood to strike or waiting for the right time.

If you find yourself frequently giving these reasons as an excuse for putting off tasks, you need to examine your schedule activities. In all likelihood, you'll find the presence of one or more of the following factors:

- Lack of clear goals
- Underestimating the difficulty of the tasks
- Underestimating the time required to complete the tasks
- Unclear standards for the task outcomes
- Feeling as the tasks are imposed on you from outside
- Too ambiguous tasks

And there are also many connections with:

- Underdeveloped decision making skills
- Fear of failure or fear of success
- Perfectionism

Avoiding procrastination is as simple as developing good decision making skills and techniques. You can begin developing good decision making skills by taking three steps. First, identify the purpose of your decision. What's the problem and why do you need to solve it? Next, gather the information you need to solve the problem and come up with possible solutions. After evaluating each option in terms of possible consequences, decide which alternative is best.

The only thing left to do is to put your decision into action and stick with it.

Special Time Management Issues

Do you find yourself frequently commenting that you can't stick to a schedule because something always pops up?

This is actually a common hurdle and none of us are immune to these. The difference between individuals who make a time management program work, and those who fall victim to these issues, is learning to identify common time wasters and handle them appropriately.

Take a look below at the list of most common reasons for reducing effectiveness.

- Interruptions - telephone
- Interruptions - personal visitors
- Meetings
- Unclear communication
- Inadequate technical knowledge
- Unclear objectives and priorities
- Lack of planning
- Stress and fatigue
- Inability to say "No"
- Personal disorganization
- Tasks you should have let someone else handle
- Procrastination and indecision
- Acting with incomplete information
- Dealing with team members
- Crisis management (fire fighting)

Before we explore the ways to deal with these issues, let's look at why they create such a problem.

Lack of priorities and objectives is perhaps one of the easiest ways to waste time. Without a clear map of where you want to go, you'll get nowhere.

Attempting to take on too much will only result in projects that are only partially completed and leave you with a feeling of failure.

Everyone has to deal with people who drop in at the last minute or try to impose their own agenda on your already packed schedule. Learning how to deal with these types of people situations is one of the best ways you can get a handle on your schedule and learn to manage your time effectively.

Delegation isn't just for corporate executives. Everyone needs to learn how to effectively delegate. The problem is that many people dislike delegating because they are afraid that someone else won't do the task nearly as well as they would. Ask yourself if someone else could do the job at least as well as 80% as you would. If your answer is yes, you should delegate it.

Do you ever find that you waste precious minutes, even hours, looking for important items? While college living isn't conducive to wide open spaces, the more clutter you can eliminate the more effective you will be at handling all your tasks.

Procrastination is one of the biggest time thieves. Try to avoid putting off your tasks and get in the habit of making decisions instead of putting them off.

One simple word can help to eliminate a significant amount of you stress: "No!" Far too often people take on too much because they're too nice or too shy to simply say "No!" Remember that there is nothing wrong with this word; in a sense, it can be savior of your sanity.

Below are some tips on how you can get a handle on these time wasters in order to better manage your time.

- As soon as you possibly can, define your goals and objectives. This is one of the most common traits of the most successful people in the world.
- The most important question you can always ask yourself is, "Right now; what is the most important way I can utilize my time?" This question will help you to focus on important tasks and avoid spending time on tasks that will get you nowhere.
- Always have a plan. Make it a point to review your plans frequently and update them accordingly as changes occur. Always keep a balance between planning and doing.
- You can't put an end to all problems, but good time management will enable you to respond appropriately and be flexible enough to ensure that even major problems won't completely derail your goals.
- On your daily to do list, make sure that you have accounted for potential interruptions.

Assign a deadline to each task and estimate how much time you anticipate each task will require. If you know that you frequently get derailed by certain interruptions; try to plan for them.

For many college students, the effort of trying maintain a healthy balance between their coursework, their home life, and a job is simply too much. You can delegate the household tasks that you are responsible for to other individuals. In order for this to work well, you need to take the following steps:

- Teach the person how to do the job, including any shortcuts that you may be aware of that can make the job go easier and faster.
- Have the best tools, supplies, and equipment for doing the job.
- Consider what household work a person already does.
- Never re-do a job (unless health and/or safety is threatened). If you do, you'll get the job back and in the end you'll ultimately be wasting more time than you're saving.
- Realize others may not meet your standards, but if you have truly given up the job, accept that your standards no longer apply. Generally speaking; if someone else can accomplish the job at least as well as 80% of the way you could handle it, then that's good enough.
- Never forget to say thank-you.

The final option would be to hire someone to handle the work for you. For most college students even hiring a maid to come in twice a week is far too expensive; however, you might consider other solutions that can help to lighten your load without breaking your wallet. For example, what about asking a local teenager to drop by every two weeks to give the place a good once over? That won't be exorbitantly expensive and you'll both benefit.

If you are responsible for the preparation of any portion of your meals, there are also some tips you can implement that will help you to save time in this area as well.

One of the best ways to do this is to implement a rotating menu system. You may choose to use either complete meals, including side dishes; on this menu or stick with hearty main dishes. Make a master shopping list for all the ingredients needed and keep it handy so that you can check off items as you run out of them.

To avoid wasting time with numerous weekly shopping trips, plan for only one large shopping trip each month. You can save even more time by cooking meals in large quantities and freezing the leftovers to create meals that can be warmed up in just a matter of minutes.

Clothing and laundry can also be dealt with in such a way as to free up a little more of your time. Simplify laundry by using baskets and hampers that have been labeled or color coded for washing machine settings. Keep the laundry near your laundry facilities to keep from having to track it down. To speed up the process of putting away completed laundry, get in the habit of moving laundry from the dryer to baskets that have been labeled so you can easily and quickly put them away.

House cleaning can also tend to sneak up on you. Try setting aside Sunday as your day for taking care of these matters. Get your room mates involved. Set up a house rule that everyone is responsible for picking up their own room.

Take the plunge and keep multiple sets of cleaning supplies in separate locations throughout the house so that no one has the excuse of not being able to locate the right cleaner in order to take care of a mess as it occurs.

Meetings

Meetings are often times a necessary evil; regardless of where you happen to be in your life. In college, you'll find that you often get caught up in meetings for study groups and extra-curricular activities.

Since eliminating meetings altogether isn't an option try to get more out of them by using the following tips.

If you're responsible for running meetings, check out the following ideas:

1. **Hold meetings only when trigger events occur.**
   Contrary to popular opinion, it is really not necessary to hold regular meetings when there is absolutely no reason to do so.

2. **Use the Agenda Effectively**
   The agenda of the meeting shows the aim of the meeting, and points of discussion in priority order - effectively it is a To Do List for the meeting. The agenda can help you to stop wanderers from drifting away from the subject at hand and ensure that everyone is fully prepared. So avoid the catch-all A.O.B. (Any Other Business) and replace with A.O.N.B. (Any Other Notified Business).

3. **Setting the time of the meeting**
   Keep in mind that the time when you schedule your meeting can best be determined by the habits of those who attend the meeting. For example; if you notice that the attendees frequently drone on and on; set the meeting for a time of time of day when everyone is anxious to either return home or get back to another activity.

Increase the productivity of meetings by only bringing in the number of people that are necessary to make it a success. Inviting additional people will only lead to increased discussion and consequently, wasted time.

Even if you are not responsible for running meetings, you can still exercise some control over it to maximize the experience. See the following tips:

- Always be on time, and present only if you are needed
- Be well prepared and briefed on your contribution

- Remain attentive to the discussion so that your contribution does not repeat someone else's
- Be involved in the discussion

Using Waiting Time

As much as we try to avoid it and as much as we plan, life is going to involve a certain amount of waiting. For most people, this time is often viewed as wasted time. It does not have to be wasted time if you learn to use it effectively.

- Always confirm your appointment the day before.
- Do not arrive more than 5 minutes early.
- Always have something with you to work on during unavoidable delays.

Do you find that your plans are often interrupted by a call from mom? Instead of waiting for her to call you when you're in the middle of trying to study for an exam, plan for this and pick up the phone and call her instead.

To make sure that you do not spend more time than you can afford on phone calls, set a specific time limit for the amount of time you can spend on the phone call. Also, try developing notes of what you intend to say or find out during your call and then stick to them.

Keep yourself from feeling deprived of much needed phone time with your parents, friends or long-distance boy- or girlfriend, allot a time during the weekend or the day when your schedule is mostly free. That way, you get your necessary class work done and still have the chance for a once-a-week catching up with your loved ones.

Never give into the pressure to be placed on hold. Instead, ask for a time when you can call back or leave your name and telephone number for them to return your call. The same applies when an individual is not able to take your call.

If you're on a deadline and can only spend a certain amount of time on the phone; let the person on the other end of the line know that up front.

Avoid the scramble of trying to find haphazardly written messages by keeping a pen and pad by the telephone.

To effectively deal with drop in visitors, try the following suggestions: as soon as the visitor arrives, establish why they've come to see you. Some people can waste an hour or more of your time before they ever get around to explaining the real reason why they dropped by. Few people stop by just to chat.

When you answer the door, remain standing. This almost forces the other person to remain standing and prevents them from 'settling' in.

Similar to the tip for dealing with phone calls; explain to the visitor that you only have a specific amount of time to dedicate to this conversation. Avoid engaging in small talk.

Review: Developing Time Management Skills

As mentioned throughout this book, there are numerous techniques and tools that you can utilize to take control of time. Below we will review the most pertinent of these techniques. This will help you to develop a clear idea of how you can efficiently manage your time.

Estimating the Cost of your Time

Many people fail to realize how much inefficiently handling their time can actually cost them. They assume that if they are not actively employed in an outside job, their time is their own. They fail to calculate the real cost of wasting time.

By estimating the cost of your time, you can assess whether you are spending your time profitably and gauge whether you need to make necessary changes.

In the corporate world, this is done by calculating how much your time costs each year in terms of salary, payroll taxes and even the cost for the office space where you work. Other expenses such as equipment, various expenses and administrative support are also tallied in.

When you're a college student, this can be a little more difficult but it can still be done. Add up the amount of financial aid that you receive each year as well as the amount of any loans that you or your parents have taken out for the cost of your education. Add your tallies according to the amount of money you receive for your education on an annual basis.

The next step is to figure the amount of money you think you should earn from your activity.

To this figure add a 'guesstimate' of the amount of profit you should generate by your activity. Begin by estimating the amount of time you spend on your activities per year. For example; if you spend roughly 8 hours per day on school activities over 200 days each year that equates to 1,500 hours per year.

Now, it is time to calculate an hourly rate. This will tell you how much your time is worth. Are your surprised at the amount?

Be sure to keep this amount in mind when you are faced with having to make a decision regarding whether to tackle a task or not. Based on the expected yield of task, do you think you would be spending your time wisely or wasting it?

Creating To-Do Lists

A to-do list is considered one of the best ways to quickly and easily manage your time. A to do list gives you the opportunity to consolidate all the tasks you must accomplish in one location. However, a to-do list must also be prioritized, with the tasks listed in order of importance so that you can take care of them first.

Preparing a to-do list is not at all difficult. It involves simply writing down the activities and task that you must accomplish. When you run across complex or large tasks, simplify them by breaking them down into manageable chunks.

After this is accomplished, you can then begin to prioritize the tasks from those that you consider to be very important to those that are unimportant at this time. You may use either a numerical or alphabetical system in order to denote importance.

Once this is done, review your list to insure that you have a proper balance. If you find that too many tasks appear to have a high priority you may need to move less important tasks to a lower priority.

Scheduling Projects

Deadlines are often the impetus that either drive people to get busy or pour more stress on top of an already simmering fire. If you find that you frequently leave your work until the last minute, your final product will have numerous errors as a result. You will most likely benefit from learning how to better schedule projects.

The first is to make sure that you understand what needs to be done and then begin breaking the project down into smaller sections. Next, estimate the amount of time that will be required for each task and allow plenty of time to review your progress. This type of monitoring system will allow you to quickly respond to problems as they occur rather than realizing at the last minute that you do not have enough time to complete the project.

Since there are no absolutes to any situation in life, there will always be at least one situation in which you run across an impossible deadline. There are several ways in which you can handle such a situation. You can choose to have the deadline extended, obtain additional resources, ask to have the final product defined to something you can actually accomplish or let the person in charge of the project know early on that you are experiencing difficulties.

Understanding Where Your Time Goes

There is an old cliché that says time flies when you're having fun. The same can also be true when you're pressed to the wall for a deadline. If you find that you frequently encounter a pressing deadline with no idea where the allotted time for the project went, it is a good idea to begin keeping track of how you use your time.

This can be done by using a weekly schedule to keep track of how use each hour of your waking day. This may seem a little mundane at first, but the result of such a personal assessment can be both enlightening and surprising.

After you have conducted such an assessment, it is time to learn from the research you have gathered. This is where putting the information you learn into use can begin to truly make a difference in how you manage your time. For example; if you discovered through your personal assessment that you typically sleep eight hours each night, then you will also learn this gives you 112 hours per week to accomplish all your tasks and activities.

Now, this sounds like a lot of time but you must keep in mind that everything must be crammed into those 112 hours including eating, doing your laundry, attending to your personal hygiene, attending class, spending time with friends and even time unwinding in front of the TV. Absolutely everything must be accounted for in your schedule.

The sample schedule below will help you to learn how to best use this tool.

Activities	Hours per Day	Total Number of Days	Total Hours per Week
On average; how many hours do you sleep during a 24 hour time period? Be sure to include your average nightly sleep as well as naps.			
On average; how many hours per day do you require for grooming?			
On average; how many hours per day do you spend on meals? Do not forget to include any time required to prepare the food and clean-up afterwards.			
How much time do you spend each day traveling to			

and from class? Do not forget to add in the amount of time it takes to find a parking spot and walk to class.			
How many hours per day do you spend on errands such as shopping, picking up dry cleaning, fueling your car, etc?			
How many hours per day do you spend on activities such as student clubs, church, etc?			
If you also work; approximately how many hours per day do you work?			
How many hours per day do you spend in class?			
How many hours per day do you spend on entertainment such as visiting with friends, watching TV, going out, etc?			

When making an assessment you must be completely honest with yourself. By analyzing this type of weekly schedule you can begin to plan your activities more efficiently and avoid last minute cramming.

The key to making time management work is to take the time to continually update your schedule. If necessary, make a point to pull an hour out of your schedule to enter pertinent data such as due dates for papers, exams, etc.

When scheduling your activities make sure you do not fall into the trap of being overbooked. When you schedule too much, you put yourself at risk for impending disaster when events beyond your control occur. For example, if you wait until the last minute to type your mid-semester paper because you've had several other activities that have required attention, you could create serious trouble for yourself when your computer crashes.

The general rule of thumb here is to only plan for about 50% of your time. This may not sound like a lot, but when you stop and thing about the number of interruptions and emergencies that can sneak up and destroy your well laid plans, you'll be glad you built flexibility into your schedule.

Some Final Tips

Before you start on any project, it is important to make sure that you first understand the exact nature and requirements of the assignment or project. If you have any questions, ask them before you begin working instead of putting them off until later.

If you happen to be working on the assignment in a group setting, ensure that everyone in the group fully understands the task at hand.

Start your scheduling of the assignment by listing all tasks you must accomplish to complete the project.

Only after you have listed the task, should you begin to prioritize them. Mark them in order of importance, writing a new list if necessary. Make sure you allot a reasonable amount of time to complete the tasks.

If necessary, delegate responsibilities. This is especially true when working in a group. Do not try to take it all on yourself. Divide up tasks equally and fairly.

After you have finished the planning phase, it is time to get started. When you have finished each individual task, be sure to cross it off your to-do list. Do not allow yourself to become distracted by other activities or tasks until you have completed the ones at hand.

In the college environment, it can be very tempting to try to work with your friends. This should only be done if you can do it effectively. If you find yourself getting up caught in chatter about items that are unrelated to your assignment, it is time to move to a private work location.

Research time can be an easy way to waste significant blocks of time. Avoid this by knowing what you are looking for. When doing research, avoid wasting time by knowing exactly what you are trying to find.

Avoid procrastination by following these tips:

- Do not procrastinate in getting started. Just do it.
- Do not be a perfectionist.
- If you find yourself putting off a task because it is boring, just go ahead and get it done so you do not have to deal with it any longer.
- Do not put things off until the last minute.

Planning for Good Health

Not taking care of your health can have serious consequences in terms of destroying your plans. Get started on the right path by having a good breakfast each and every morning. If you have a tendency to start running down by mid-morning, pack a healthy snack to revive your energy. Avoid large lunches as this can lead to lower energy levels in the afternoon.

Take time to rest. Plan for occasional ten or fifteen minute breaks in order to restore your thought processes and energy.

Do not allow yourself to become a victim of burn out by committing to more things than you can reasonably accomplish. Learn to say "No!" and mean it.

If you have a tendency to be a perfectionist, learn to curb those tendencies or suffer the consequences. Perfectionists tend to be the worst at effective time management, because good is never quite good enough. Avoid putting unneeded effort into a project.

Adjusting to university life isn't easy by any stretch of the imagination. In fact, there will be some days when you feel that survival is your top priority. During these times, it is okay to realize that you need to let go of everything else in order to just get through those brief time periods.

Be willing to commit to a regular review of your schedule in order to determine whether you may need to reconsider the amount of time you spend on certain activities.

Appendix A

	Monday	Tuesday	Wednesday	Thursday	Friday	Saturday	Sunday
7-8	Dress & Breakfast	Dress & Breakfast	Dress & Breakfast	Dress & Breakfast	Dress & Breakfast		
8-9	Comp & Lit		Comp & Lit			Dress & Breakfast	Dress & Breakfast
9-10		Sociology		Sociology			
10-11	Spanish		Spanish				
11-12		Biology		Biology	Biology Lab		
12-1							
1-2							
2-3						Biology Study Group	
3-4							
4-5	Taekwondo		Taekwondo		Taekwondo		
5-6							
6-7	Dinner	Dinner	Dinner	Dinner	Dinner	Dinner	Dinner
7-8							
8-9							
9-10							
11-12							

Appendix B

Table 1.1

Weekly Schedule	Monday	Tuesday	Wednesday	Thursday	Friday	Saturday	Sunday
7-8							
8-9							
9-10							
10-11							
11-12							
12-1							
1-2							

2-3	3-4	4-5	5-6	6-7	7-8	8-9

Table 1.2

Long Term Planner
__/__/__ to __/__/__

Week of	Monday	Tuesday	Wednesday	Thursday	Friday	Saturday	Sunday
/							
/							
/							
/							
/							
/							

Table 1.3

Four-year Planning

	Fall	Winter	Spring	Summer
1st Year				
2nd Year				
3rd Year				
4th Year				

Appendix C

In this appendix you will find more forms and tools that can help you to get better organized and be more efficient in managing your time.

Itinerary

Name:	Date:
Location:	

CALL	ITEM	RESULT	RESCHEDULE
Name: Address:			
Name: Address:			
Name: Address:			
Name: Address:			
Name: Address:			

Name: Address:			
Name: Address:			
NOTES			

Time Log

Name: _____

Date: _____

Start Time	Activity	Priority	Duration

To do list

Date	Priority	Activity	Start Date	Due Date
	_1 _2 _3			
	_1 _2 _3			
	_1 _2 _3			
	_1 _2 _3			
	_1 _2 _3			
	_1 _2 _3			

Important Date Sheet

Course Title and #	Professor Name	Papers		Papers, Quizzes		Quizzes, Tests		Tests, Special Assignments	
		Due Date	Grade	Due Date	Grade	Due Date	Grade	Due Date	Grade
1st									
2nd									
3rd									
4th									

Long-Term Goal:
1.
2.
3.

Intermediate Goals:
1.
2.
3.
4.

Short-Term Goals (Present):
1.
2.
3.
4.
5.

Activities	Hours per Day	Total Number of Days	Total Hours per Week
On average; how many hours do you sleep during a 24 hour time period? Be sure to include your average nightly sleep as well as naps.			
On average; how many hours per day do you require for grooming? On average; how many hours per day do you spend on meals? Do not forget to include any time required to prepare the food and clean-up afterwards.			
How much time do you spend each day traveling to and from work? Do not forget to add in the amount of time it takes to find a parking spot and walk to your office.			

How many hours per day do you spend on errands such as shopping, picking up dry cleaning, fueling your car, etc?			
How many hours per day do you spend on activities such as hobby clubs, church, etc?			
How many hours per day do you spend at work?			
How many hours per day do you spend entertaining guests for work?			
How many hours per day do you spend on entertainment such as visiting with friends, watching tv, going out, etc?			

Daily Activity Guide

A. Priority Level One

     1.
     2.
     3.
     4.
     5.
     6.
     7.
     8.
     9.
     10.

B. Priority Level Two

     1.
     2.
     3.
     4.
     5.
     6.
     7.
     8.
     9.
     10.

C. Priority Level Three

1.
2.
3.
4.
5.
6.
7.
8.
9.
10.

To-do List

Date: _____

Done	Task

Note:

_____

_____

_____

_____

Weekly Menu

Menu for the week of _____

	Breakfast	Lunch	Dinner
Monday			
Tuesday			
Wednesday			
Thursday			
Friday			
Saturday			
Sunday			

Items not in the menu:

_____

_____

_____

_____

_____

_____

_____

_____

_____

Chore List

Chores for the week of _____

Name	Day	Chore
		Wash car
		Clean closets
		Clean drawers
		Clean windows and glass doors
		Clean mirrors
		Clean garage
		Mow the yard
		Dust furniture
		Change linens
		Wash clothes
		Do dishes
		Vacuum floors / Sweep / Mop
		Clean bathrooms

Monthly shopping list
For the Month Of:_____

Household Items

_____
_____
_____
_____
_____

Yard and Garden Items

_____
_____
_____
_____
_____

Family/Birthday/Anniversary Gifts

_____
_____
_____
_____
_____

Clothes/Shoes

_____
_____
_____
_____
_____

Pets

_____
_____
_____
_____
_____

Auto

_____
_____
_____
_____
_____

School Supplies

_____
_____
_____
_____
_____

Special notes:

_____
_____
_____

Grocery List

Breads/Cereals

- [ ] Sandwich bread
- [ ] French Bread
- [ ] Dinner Rolls
- [ ] Hoagie Rolls
- [ ] Pita Bread
- [ ] Flour Tortillas
- [ ] Corn Tortillas
- [ ] Cereal
- [ ] Oatmeal
- [ ] Biscuits
- [ ] Pancake Mix
- [ ] Muffin Mix
- [ ] Cake Mix
- [ ] Brownie Mix
- [ ] Pie Crusts
- [ ] Cookie Mix
- [ ] Cookies

Dairy

- [ ] Milk

Fresh Fruits &Vegetables

- [ ] Lettuce
- [ ] Tomato
- [ ] Carrots
- [ ] Green Beans
- [ ] Potatoes
- [ ] Broccoli
- [ ] Spinach
- [ ] Mushrooms
- [ ] Onions
- [ ] Cauliflower
- [ ] Radishes
- [ ] Corn
- [ ] Avocados
- [ ] Fruit
- [ ] _____
- [ ] _____

Desserts

- [ ] Cake
- [ ] Pie

Frozen Foods & Meat

- [ ] Chicken
- [ ] Beef
- [ ] Pork
- [ ] Lunchmeats
- [ ] _____
- [ ] _____
- [ ] _____

Non Perishables

- [ ] Beans
- [ ] Rice
- [ ] Pasta
- [ ] Canned Soup
- [ ] Canned Vegetables
- [ ] Canned Meat
- [ ] Canned Fruit

Other

- [ ] Detergent
- [ ] Dishwasher Soap
- [ ] Bleach

- [ ] Butter
- [ ] Eggs
- [ ] Sour Cream
- [ ] Whipping Cream
- [ ] Creamer
- [ ] Cottage Cheese
- [ ] Yogurt
- [ ] Cheddar Cheese
- [ ] American Cheese
- [ ] Swiss Cheese
- [ ] Mozarella
- [ ] Velveeta

Beverages
- [ ] Coffee
- [ ] Tea
- [ ] Juices
- [ ] Sodas
- [ ] Mixes

- [ ] Pudding
- [ ] Cheesecake
- [ ] Brownies
- [ ] Donuts

Condiments
- [ ] Mustard
- [ ] Mayonnaise
- [ ] Pickles
- [ ] Catsup
- [ ] Olives
- [ ] Dressings
- [ ] Jelly/Jam
- [ ] Peanut Butter

Baking Goods
- [ ] Flour
- [ ] Sugar
- [ ] Yeast
- [ ] Baking Powder
- [ ] Corn Starch

- [ ] Disinfectant
- [ ] Cleanser
- [ ] Pet Supplies
- [ ] Napkins
- [ ] Paper Towels
- [ ] Toilet Paper
- [ ] Kleenex
- [ ] Toothpicks
- [ ] Paper Plates
- [ ] Paper Cups